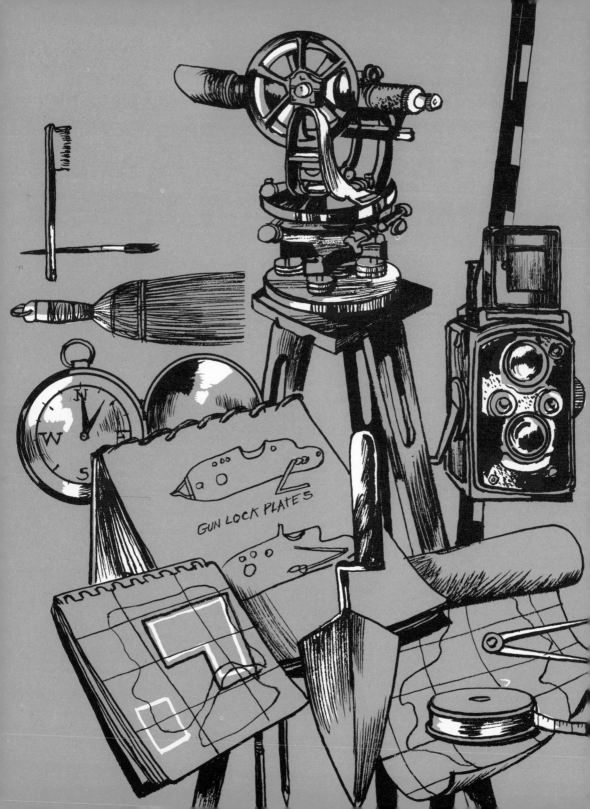

GUN LOCK PLATES

The BIG DIG

A Frontier Fort Comes to Life

Written and Illustrated by

DIRK GRINGHUIS

 THE DIAL PRESS   **New York**

TO

DR. MOREAU S. MAXWELL

Head archaeologist on the first big dig.
Museum, Michigan State University

WITH SPECIAL THANKS TO
W. S. Woodfill
and the other members of the
Mackinac Island State Park Commission

AND TO

Dr. E. T. Petersen,
Director of Historic Projects,
whose efforts have made these plans for restoration a reality.

At the northern tip of Michigan's lower peninsula stood a fort. Partly rebuilt, the old stockade of pointed logs enclosed a fairly level stretch of ground and three log buildings. The fort was deserted.

9

On the inside a raised platform ringed the two palisades facing the beach. Rough steps led up to gun platforms where block-houses, sturdy corner buildings above the walls, had once stood. Square-cut holes for muskets, eyeless now, looked out across the Straits of Mackinac. Where once the long canoe of the Indian had traveled with the voyageur's bateau, or wooden boat, long ships passed and repassed.

Ore boats, tankers, freighters, sailing yachts headed down into Lake Michigan to ports in Illinois, Indiana, Wisconsin, Michigan. Others made their way up the Lake, through the Straits, then down again into Lakes Huron and Erie. Still others, carrying foreign flags, pointed their prows toward Canada and the St. Lawrence Seaway. And high above them "Big Mac," the mighty Mackinac Bridge, reached across the five miles of water, linking the two peninsulas. From the fort the mighty cables looked like spider webs, the moving automobiles like tiny toys.

The fort was Old Fort Michilimackinac (mich-ill-ih-mack-ih-naw), meaning *place of the great turtle spirits*. Built by the French some time in the early eighteenth century, it was a gathering spot for hundreds of French traders and explorers who stopped here to trade with the Indians—Chippewa, Ottawa, Sac, Potawatomi. Then in 1761 the French and Indian War was over. The victorious British took over the fort. But three years later Pontiac, the great war chief of the Indians, raised the hatchet against the intruders. And in 1763 this fort was the scene of the bloodiest massacre in Michigan history.

Now it was May, 1959. Looking to the northeast beyond the bridge, Mackinac Island (mack-ih-naw) lay like a great hump-backed turtle, whose name it bore. And high on its crest rose another fort—Fort Mackinac which *first* stood here on the mainland! How did it get to the island? History supplied the facts.

Fearing an attack from the south by American forces during the War of Independence, the British had moved the old fort across the Straits to Mackinac Island. Log by log, the church, the barracks, everything that could be hauled on the ice or carried by ship was taken across and rebuilt. And so, in 1781, Fort Michilimackinac lay deserted. In a few years nothing was left but a few rotting timbers.

Ft. MICHILIMACKINAC
A MAP by Lieut. Perkins Magra
made in 1766
MAJOR ROBT. ROGERS, Commandant

What had it originally looked like? How was it first built? When? This was the unsolved mystery since the last stockade had crumbled. What lay beneath the sand and grass where Michilimackinac had once stood?

Even the maps—some dating back to 1760—wouldn't agree. The secret lay buried. And now that the old fort was to be completely restored, the mysteries had to be solved. The Mackinac Island State Park Commission needed a detective. And in June the detective and his staff were ready.

The archaeologist in charge was Moreau S. Maxwell. His assistant, Lewis Binford, was a graduate student. His crew would come later.

Their equipment was strange for detectives. Instead of badges they carried steel tapes and notebooks. Instead of guns, whiskbrooms; instead of prowl cars, wheelbarrows. There was other gear too, a surveyor's transit, a camera, maps, compass, notebooks, shovels, trowels, hundreds of small paper sacks. Their clues were written descriptions, old maps, *artifacts,* and *potsherds* or *sherds*. Artifacts are any object showing the touch or workmanship of man, and potsherds or sherds are broken bits of pottery. Other clues would be found in the sand, clay, rocks, and soil. For these men were archaeologists, detectives of the past.

Archaeology is the scientific study of the past, the digging up of not just things but the true stories of real people! A dig is really history outdoors. It can discover how nations grew strong and how they fell. It tells what people wore, how they lived, of their weapons, houses, even their toys.

The big dig on Fort Michilimackinac began in June, 1959. The two archaeologists began to lay out the ground into sections called grids.

First they chose a datum point. This was a spot toward the edge of the dig where all measurements would start. Here a steel rod was driven into the ground. Next, using a steel tape and stakes, the entire fort area was divided into ten-foot squares, like a giant checkerboard. Each stake was marked, 0, 10, 20, 30, all the way to the end. Then the squares to the left were marked, left 10 or L 10, L 20, L 30, etc., and to the right, R 10, R 20, R 30, etc. The crew would dig in each of these squares.

Next they made a contour map. This was a map showing the height of the hills and the depth of the holes or valleys from the ground level. To do this, one man took the surveyors instrument called a transit and stood at the datum point. The other took a long rod marked off in feet and inches. The rod man placed his pole next to the first grid stake and held it straight up. The transit man sighted his instrument at the rod and read the height. With simple figuring, he could tell the height or depth of the ground at that point. This he wrote down.

Next the rod man marked the stake showing the level where the measurement was taken. They moved on to the next stake until all of the grid squares were sighted and marked. Finished, the contour or shape of the ground was known. This is the contour map. When artifacts were found, the archaeologists would know exactly at what depth they lay, because they now knew at what depth they had started to dig.

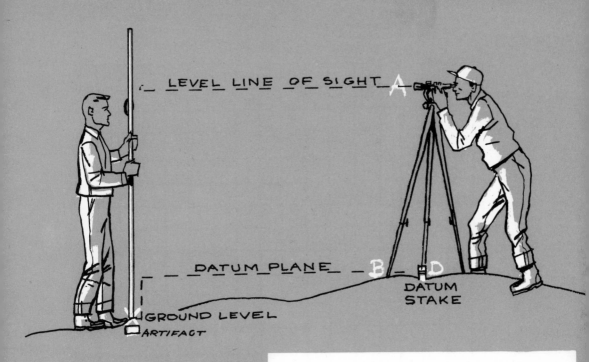

LEVEL LINE OF SIGHT A

DATUM PLANE B D

DATUM STAKE

GROUND LEVEL

ARTIFACT

HEIGHT OF SIGHT A

LESS HEIGHT OF

TRANSIT AB EQUALS

LEVEL OF GROUND X

ABOVE OR BELOW

DATUM PLANE D

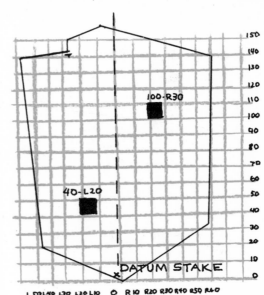

150
140
130
120
110
100
90
80
70
60
50
40
30
20
10
0

100-R30

40-L20

DATUM STAKE

L50 L40 L30 L20 L10   0   R10 R20 R30 R40 R50 R60

LEFT   RIGHT

GRID MAP

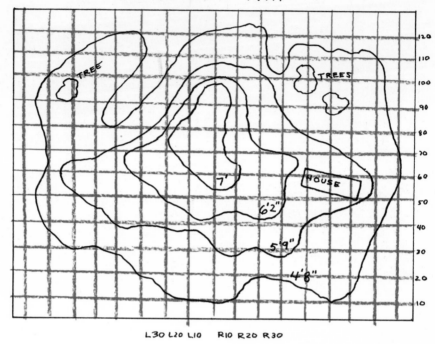

L30 L20 L10   R10 R20 R30

Now for the dig! In came the crew carrying shovels, trowels, whiskbrooms, soft brushes, needles or fine hooks, wheelbarrows, sifting screens. Two men were to dig in each square, one to move dirt and one to work the sifter.

Carefully they set to work. First the sod was peeled away and saved. All dirt was put twice through the screen sifter to rescue tiny artifacts. Then slowly, using the small trowels, three inches of dirt were removed. The walls of the square were kept straight and smooth. Now the bare ground showed the first faint patches of dark and light earth. The hunt was on.

In square L 20 a trowel clinked against metal. Gently, so as not to disturb the position of the find, the workman brushed

18

at the soil with his whiskbroom, exposing a pointed metal object. Rust-covered, it was about six inches long. Finally the object rested on a low platform of dirt. It was now *in situ,* meaning "in the place it was found." Calling the director, he stepped back, wondering.

The director knelt, studying the artifact. Next he made a careful drawing in his notebook, noted the depth, its position next to a buried pile of stone, and the type of soil. Then carefully he lifted the object, put it into a paper sack, and tagged it with the square number.

The first rule of the dig had been followed. Never move an artifact until a complete record is made!

By now, the diggers in R 30 had a find—tiny blue beads, soil-stained, the string rotted away. They were cleaned, their position noted, then put into a paper sack and tagged. If the objects were very tiny, they found their way into match boxes. Larger artifacts were photographed *in situ,* where they were found.

The digging went on, and the sifting. Pieces of cloth and gold braid, decayed and delicate as butterfly wings, more beads, bullets, and buttons were discovered.

It was sundown, and the workers straightened aching backs. But the excitement had begun.

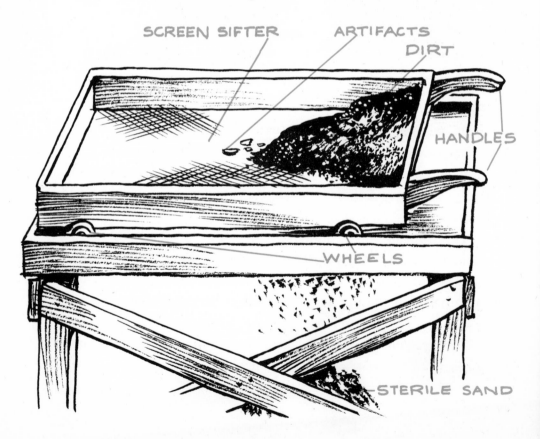

That night under a lamp the archaeologists worked until after midnight. Sorting, cleaning, labelling, they gathered the first clues, sketched a new map, and noted the place of the day's finds.

The metal piece? A lock from a British musket with the word "Bennett." English-made between 1750 and 1775. The beads? Trade beads made for the Indians in return for furs.

The first key to the mystery was here. Since no one had lived on the site since 1781, the top layers in the fort had to be late British. There lay the proof, a piece of rusted metal, fitting into known history like a piece from a jig-saw puzzle.

At sunup the dig began once more. Digging, sifting, three inches at a time, the men probed deeper. The streaks of dark earth gave way to stone foundations. To the trained eye of the archaeologist, the walls of the deepening trenches began to read like picture books.

Then, below the stones, older foundations began to appear. Dark spots of earth showed where log posts had once stood. Charred earth told of a burned-out house, pits of ashes became fireplaces. Buttons now had real meaning. Those with numbers, toward the top layers, had to be later than 1765. For it was then the British army changed the button style on the uniforms to show the number of each regiment. Pewter buttons were for enlisted men, silver buttons for the officers.

And the record grew longer. Here lay the buttons of men from the King's 8th, the 17th, and 10th, the 60th or Royal Americans.

Then there were the bits of charred cloth from 1763. And suddenly the story of the massacre seemed very real. For in 1763 Pontiac, the great war chief, had brought the tribes together. "Drive out the British," was the war cry! The war belts of wampum and the bloody hatchet carried the cry among the tribes gathering in the deep forests.

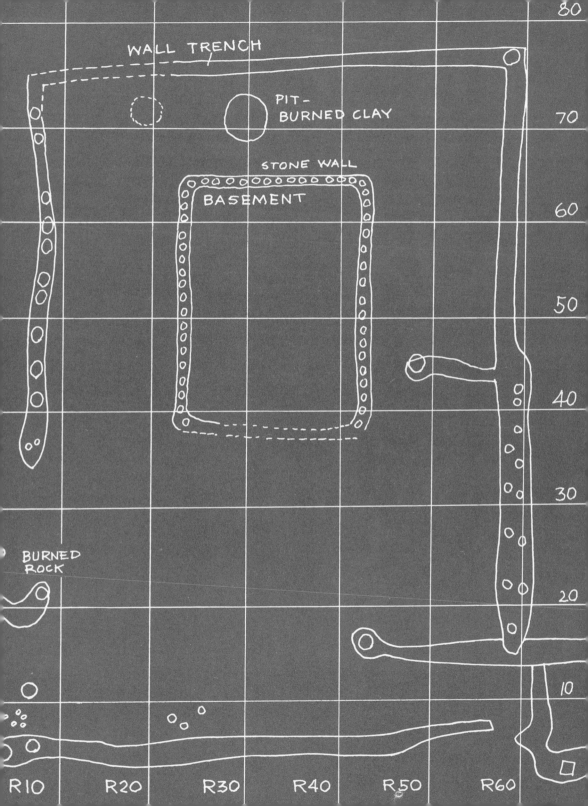

At night, holding the bits of pewter, the archaeologists could almost see the soldiers as they had once looked. There was the 60th, red-coated, white-wigged, wearing the blue cuffs and facings, white crossed belt, white leggings. And there was the 8th, in the cut-down tricornes of riflemen, shortened red jackets, canvas leggings, the uniform changed to better fit wilderness warfare.

KING'S 8th

60th. FOOT Royal Americans

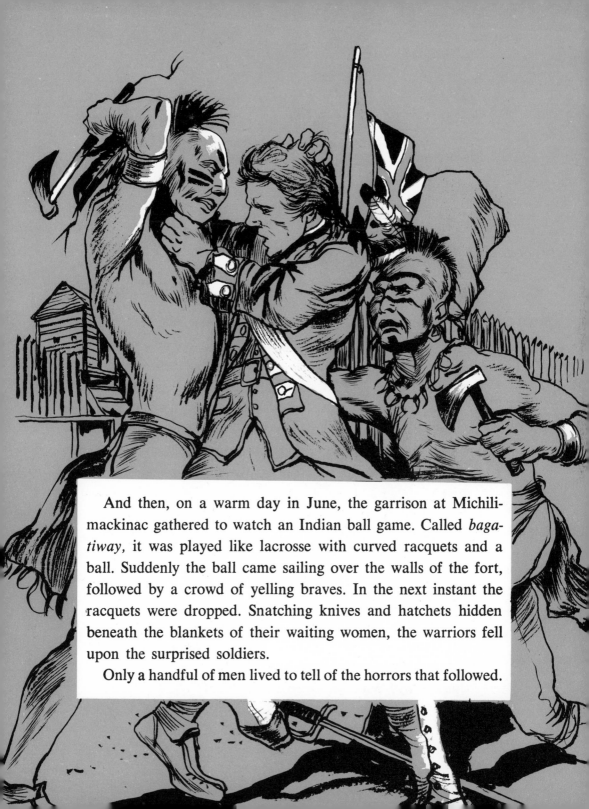

And then, on a warm day in June, the garrison at Michilimackinac gathered to watch an Indian ball game. Called *baga-
tiway,* it was played like lacrosse with curved racquets and a
ball. Suddenly the ball came sailing over the walls of the fort,
followed by a crowd of yelling braves. In the next instant the
racquets were dropped. Snatching knives and hatchets hidden
beneath the blankets of their waiting women, the warriors fell
upon the surprised soldiers.

Only a handful of men lived to tell of the horrors that followed.

Back at the dig the trenches were now five feet deep. But the picture of rock, sand, earth, one on top of another, grew cloudy. New maps were made to try and solve some of the mysteries.

Imagine you were the archaeologist. Could you read these clues? Below the second layer you found narrow streaks of dark dirt on grey sand, eight inches apart, running across four squares of the grid. Next came a six-foot square of charcoal. Then stones were revealed and, below them, pink clay with a line of round, dark spots. Several layers down there was a new line of dark spots beneath the stones, stopping at the center, then starting again. In the center section yellow sand and gravel went all the way down to the bottom of the dig. On the top layers were buttons with an "8," below them buttons reading "60." Toward the bottom were found buttons with hollow backs, and some broken clay pipes. But in the center where the yellow sand lies, there was nothing but some bones and pieces of broken china. Why? What had been here? When?

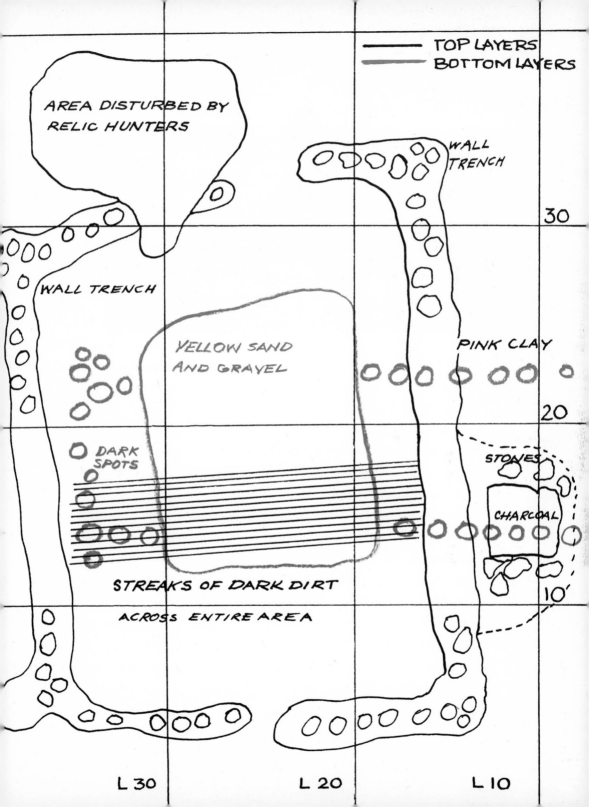

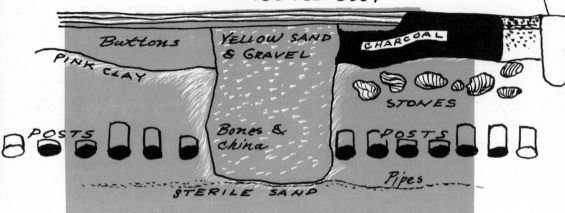

SCALE

0 1' 2' 3' 4' 5' 6'

WALL TRENCH

FLOORBOARD DUST

Buttons

YELLOW SAND & GRAVEL

CHARCOAL

PINK CLAY

STONES

POSTS

Bones & china

POSTS

Pipes

STERILE SAND

Sketching new maps, one on the other, the archaeologist found the answer. The dark strips of dirt showed where the floorboards of the building lay. The dark strips were the dust in the cracks. The charcoal square was a fireplace. In the grey sand the round, dark spots were log posts of the walls. Further down, the new line of spots showed an earlier building upon which the top one had been built. Where the posts disappeared was an old cellar shoveled full of yellow sand and gravel by the last builders so that they could build above it. And because the top layer held buttons from the 8th and 60th regiments, the building was British. The old building held hollow buttons. Only the French backed their uniform buttons with wood. This backing had rotted away. The bottom building was French. The cellar held bones from the kitchen, the china of a pattern made in England between 1750 and 1770. The British had filled in the cellar. This was an actual problem. Did you solve it?

By now the actual age of the fort began to appear. Musket parts told the maker and sometimes the year. Musket flints were of two colors and helped tell the dates. For one color was made in France, the other imported later from England. Clay pipes became calendars. Before 1715 pipe stems were bored five sixty-fourths of an inch. After 1715 they were four sixty-fourths of an inch in diameter. There was little doubt now. The French must have built between 1705 and 1715.

EARLY FRENCH HOUSE

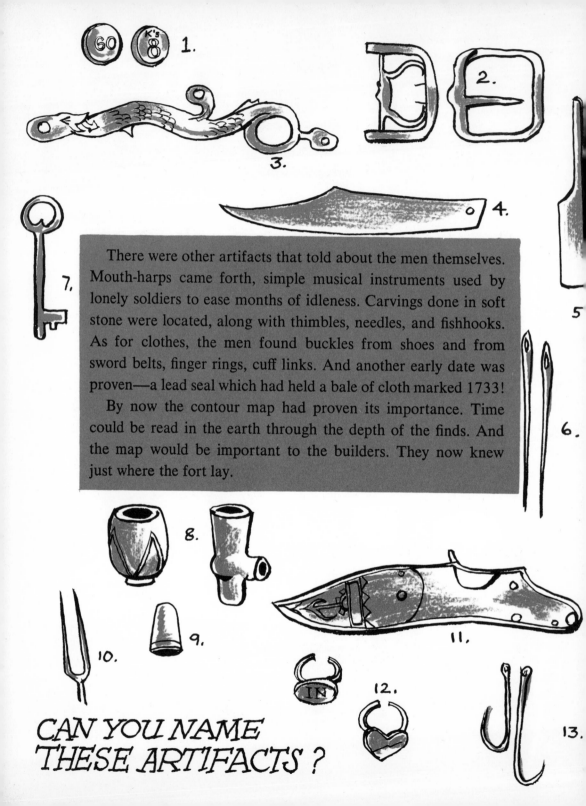

There were other artifacts that told about the men themselves. Mouth-harps came forth, simple musical instruments used by lonely soldiers to ease months of idleness. Carvings done in soft stone were located, along with thimbles, needles, and fishhooks. As for clothes, the men found buckles from shoes and from sword belts, finger rings, cuff links. And another early date was proven—a lead seal which had held a bale of cloth marked 1733!

By now the contour map had proven its importance. Time could be read in the earth through the depth of the finds. And the map would be important to the builders. They now knew just where the fort lay.

CAN YOU NAME
THESE ARTIFACTS?

BRITISH BUTTONS **1.**

BRITISH UNIFORM BUCKLES **2.**

TRADE MUSKET
L. SIDE PLATE - BRITISH   **3.**

4.

FRENCH CLASP KNIFE BLADE

RAZOR
5.

...EY   **7.**

6.

But there were disappointments too. A pit dug by some thoughtless relic hunters had destroyed one-half of the commanding officer's house. Artifacts found there were worthless because they were out of place. That night Dr. Maxwell shook his head. If the people who found artifacts would just leave them alone and report the find to their museum or historical society. Careless digging could destroy centuries of history with one stroke of a shovel!

NEEDLES

PIPE BOWLS

8.

10.   **9.**

THIMBLE

MUSKET LOCK PLATE
11.

JESUIT RINGS

FISH
HOOKS

TABLE FORK

12.

13.

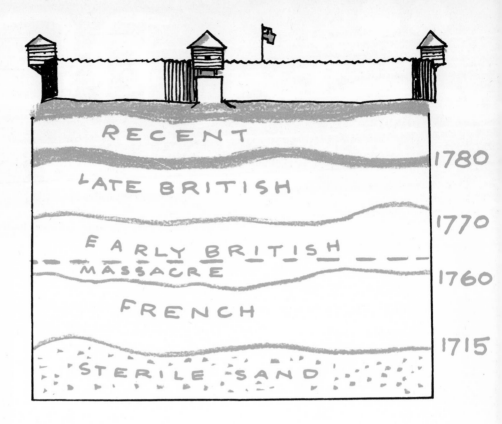

RECENT — 1780
LATE BRITISH — 1770
EARLY BRITISH
MASSACRE — 1760
FRENCH
— 1715
STERILE SAND

And now, with only one-eighth of the fort dug up, the days were growing short. The sun which still blazed above the backs of the workmen sank earlier beyond the waves of Lake Michigan. And the Straits turned grey with the coming of September storms.

Then one day the old stockade was empty once more. Even the piles of dirt were gone. For the trained archaeologist leaves the scene of his dig just as he found it. Instead of sweating men, chipmunks raced across the newly smoothed ground. But to the archaeologist, with his notes, his pictures, sketches, artifacts, and maps, the filled-in earth was as clear as any photograph.

TRADE BEADS

SHOE
BUCKLES

Back at the museum when the classifying, the reports, the numbered artifacts, and the maps were reorganized, the two scientists realized what they had found. Only one-eighth of the fort had been searched. But there, in front of them, lay the most thoroughly proven collection of early French frontier fort artifacts in the world!

It was time for others to begin their work. Plans, lists of materials, detailed drawings of the soldier's barracks, a French trader's house were started. Later there would be a guard house, a church, powder magazine, King's storehouse.

MUSKET
HAMMERS

LOCK PLATES

BONE BLANKS FOR
CLOTH-BUTTON BACKS

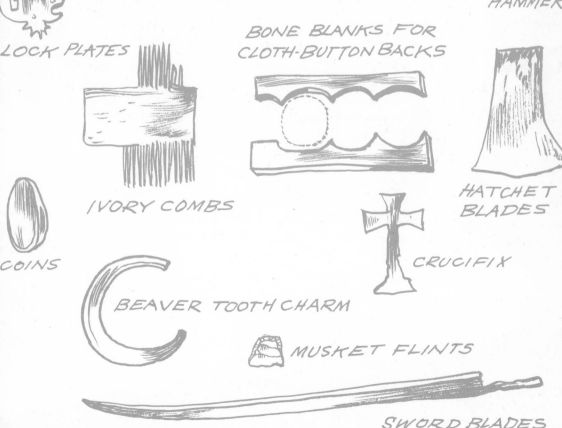

IVORY COMBS

HATCHET
BLADES

COINS

CRUCIFIX

BEAVER TOOTH CHARM

MUSKET FLINTS

SWORD BLADES

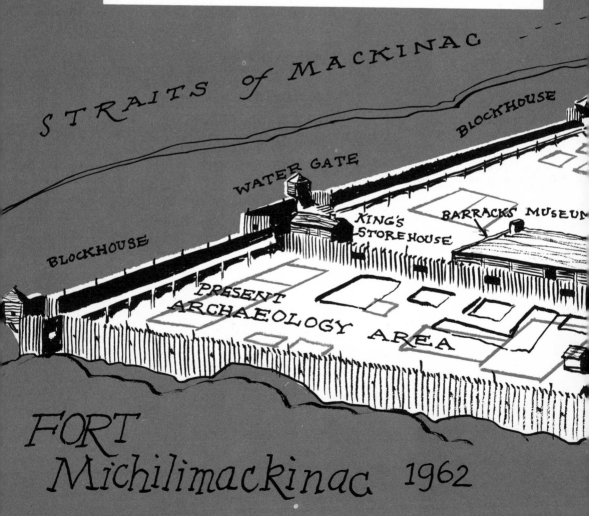

ST. IGNACE
FORT DE BUADE

MACKINAC BRIDGE

Now, on the original site, Fort Michilimackinac, though incomplete, is one of the finest frontier forts in the country. Like Fort Mackinac on Mackinac Island and Fort de Buade (still to be restored) across the Straits, Old Fort Michilimackinac will help complete the chain of history. And visitors from all over the nation will continue flocking in to places like Williamsburg, Jamestown, Forts Ticonderoga, Niagara, Snelling, Mackinac ——visitors who want to see their America as it was, to see history that has come to life!

STRAITS of MACKINAC

WATER GATE

BLOCKHOUSE

KING'S STOREHOUSE

BARRACKS MUSEUM

BLOCKHOUSE

PRESENT ARCHAEOLOGY AREA

FORT Michilimackinac 1962

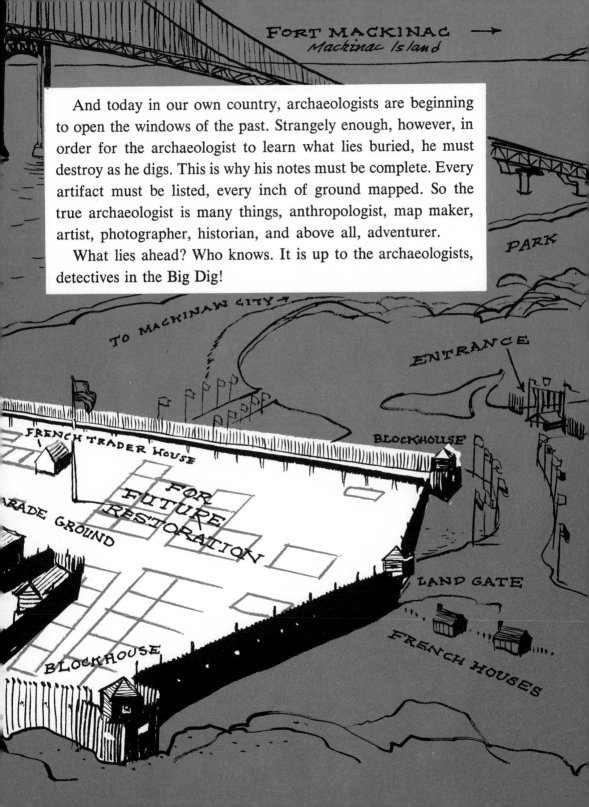

And today in our own country, archaeologists are beginning to open the windows of the past. Strangely enough, however, in order for the archaeologist to learn what lies buried, he must destroy as he digs. This is why his notes must be complete. Every artifact must be listed, every inch of ground mapped. So the true archaeologist is many things, anthropologist, map maker, artist, photographer, historian, and above all, adventurer.

What lies ahead? Who knows. It is up to the archaeologists, detectives in the Big Dig!

PARK

TO MACKINAW CITY →

ENTRANCE

FRENCH TRADER HOUSE

BLOCKHOUSE

FOR FUTURE RESTORATION

PARADE GROUND

LAND GATE

BLOCKHOUSE

FRENCH HOUSES

Appendix

The Big Dig at Fort Michilimackinac is only one of many archaeological expeditions going on today. In other sections of America and the world men are at work with shovel and whiskbroom, patiently unraveling the mysteries of yesterday.

Today's archaeologist requires special knowledge in many fields. Most universities offer courses necessary for this training. Anthropology is one, the study of man's development and customs; ethnology, the races of man; geology, the study of rocks and the earth. And while methods of digging are much the same everywhere, most students specialize in that part of the world which interests them the most, whether it is the Far East or the early Indian in America's great southwest.

One of the newest tools in the search for yesterday is the aqualung. With it the modern scientist can find history at the sea bottom or underneath rivers.

Archaeology also needs people with other skills—historians, architects, surveyors, chemists, artists, photographers, construction men, even trained nurses. And no matter how they may reach their "dig," by camel back, or jeep, by airplane or mule back, adventure and mystery awaits them everywhere.

SEE: *Archeology As A Career,*
           #4343, SMITHSONIAN INSTITUTE,
           WASHINGTON, D. C.

       A Guide to Archeological Field Methods, Heizer
           NATIONAL PRESS, PALO ALTO, CALIFORNIA

       Excavation at Fort Michilimackinac,
           Maxwell and Binford,
    THE MUSEUM, MICHIGAN STATE UNIVERSITY